TO LIVE LIKE A KING

To Live Like A King

THE FINANCIAL SUCCESS GUIDE

Luke Schoemaker

This guide is dedicated to all the family and friends that helped me find my path and to all of you who are about to find your own way "To Live Like A King."

Contents

Introduction

To live like a king! A classic phrase that says so much with so few words. Unlike so many books these days that say so little in so many. The object of this book is to do the opposite. The title was chosen because everyone interprets the phrase in their own way. Just as we all have our own idea of what it means to be rich or to live our dream life. The intent of this book is to help you pave your own path by showing examples of how to build a mindset of success and use the tools that will get you on the way to your dream.

I've never hit the lottery or inherited a fortune. I'm not a Certified Public Accountant or Certified Financial Planner. I'm just your average Joe that found a way for every average Joe to get on track and live the life of their dreams. I hope that by helping you create a prosperous future, you will want to share your success and help more people understand their finances.

It is said that if you take 15 minutes a day, you can learn anything: a new language, the guitar, etc. Well, what if I said it takes less than that to become a millionaire? I will show you how after the initial prep work, it will only take a few minutes each month to stay on track and prosper. The ability to plan and be good with money are skill sets that we all should strive for. People put the idea of being a millionaire on such a high pedestal that they don't even think that it is possible for them to achieve. In many cases this is why they never try. Throughout this book you will see how it is well within anyone's reach.

The first steps of building your path will be the most time consuming and will vary greatly for each individual but it is one of the most important parts of your journey. Together, we will pave this path! Starting by dreaming of where you want to be and using this book as your guide to develop the path from where you are now to get there. You will make that connection, follow your path, and by doing this claim your throne!

Once you start building on your successes and living your dream, I hope you will want to help others reach theirs. The most fulfilling thing in life for me is to help others and see them prosper. That is why I have written this book and shared these free tools on ToLiveLikeAKing.com. This is where you can find all the free tools created to help you with your personal financial journey.

OVERVIEW OF THE PATH TO COME

This journey is a six-step process to understand all aspects of your financial life and help get you to your personal finish line. "Envisioning Your Kingdom" is the start of it all. It's about finding your motives, identifying your dreams and working together to come up with your goals. Finding the drive to succeed will take some work and you will need to be honest with yourself in order to achieve your objectives. No one knows you better than yourself. As we find out where you want to be financially it is also important to figure out what motivates you! These motives will be what drives you to achieve the goals set along the way. My wife and I do this together and I strongly suggest that you do this with your partner. The most financially strong and happy couples in my life have done this and they inspired me to do the same.

Step two is "Knowing Where You Are." We will walk through the budgeting template to help you record your current financial position. Your current position is critical in developing the path to where you want to be. That brings us to step three: "Paving Your Path." This is where we lay out intermediate goals to connect the dots along the way to your final objective. Boosting your income, reducing expensive habits, and starting to formulate your budget are some examples of intermediate goals and ways that you can adjust your current position to overcome the obstacles that may be holding you back. This provides extra cash that will feed your strategy to meet your goals, drive down bad debt, and build your savings. This is how we start "Earning Your Throne" in step four.

After paying off bad debt and saving for emergencies it's time for step five "Reaching for the Crown." The crown is your end goal and keeping that in mind will help you stay motivated to keep reaching for your goals and investing in the future. Staying motivated by using standard and personal checkpoints as intermediate goals will keep the end in sight making it easier to keep pushing toward your final destination.

The final step is "Expanding Your Empire." Step

six is where we discuss best practices and alternate ways to continue building your legacy. We will go over investment strategies and how they should change as you age. The long-term goal is financial independence in retirement. Many people don't understand what financial independence is but this is the key to the dream that we all want. The ability to do what you want because you can not because you have to. The goal is to figure out how you can live off of your investments and have them support your dream. It is the ability to do anything you want, without worry if it will work out or if it will ever make a profit. You will be living off the investments and the rest is up to you.

Casey and Ashton

Throughout our guide you will see how Casey and Ashton go from step one to six together. Their example will show how each step changed their financial wellbeing. Casey and Ashton are newlyweds in their mid-twenties and both want to retire at or before the age of 60. Casey is a postal worker and Ashton is a bartender that does some freelance work as a painter. They just started trying to invest, have minimal savings, and are paying off multiple debts.

WHERE I STARTED

You may be looking at me and asking yourself how am I going to teach you to retire financially independent, build generational wealth, and leave a legacy for your family. The short answer is that I have struggled many times in my life. Finding out the hard way was how I learned what not to do as well as how to fix it. Now my wife and I are well on our way to a million-dollar net worth. Our current focus is on being multi-millionaires and retiring before the age of 50. I want everyone to see how simple changes can make an immense impact!

These steps can be used by anyone to get on track to their own goals. Freeing you to live the life you always dreamed of and not worry about running out of money in retirement. This is not a get rich quick scheme. This is just a simple way to use the tools to help you get financially secure.

People learn in many different ways which can be summed up in two categories: personal experience or mentorship. The key is to absorb as much as possible from others' experiences so you don't make the same mistakes. If you want the long version of how I learned my lesson continue on. If you want to get right to it, skip right to step one "Envisioning Your Kingdom."

I grew up in a lower middle-class family in a small town in Pennsylvania. They paid their bills and had a mortgage but didn't have a lot of spare cash for extras. We were far from poverty but money was a central focus. Many of the lessons I look back on involve how to save or not to spend excessively. Needless to say, this has made a big impact on my life. I was always focused on how to make money and work for what I wanted. As a small child I would do my brother's chores and he would pay me in the trading cards. As I got older, I cut the grass in the summer and stacked wood in the winter. I washed dishes at a local pub and worked seasonal jobs. I worked for anyone that offered me a job. Much of my focus was on how to find work so I could get the things that I wanted.

My drive for income was great but I never invested and never saved anything aside from a few thousand bucks that I spent on my first car. I continued to learn the hard way by always trying to do something more advanced before I got to learn the basics. I was always looking for a profit to be found. I looked into any type of deal or business I could do at that age and experience. Mostly did well in the things that I put effort into. Buying and selling was something I enjoyed. My mistake was that I kept investing in possessions instead of investing in myself. I continued to make similar financial decisions as a young adult.

The lowest financial moment of my life was when I was just out of college. I rented a trailer with my girlfriend at the time. We lived paycheck to paycheck and most of the time came up short. I worked throughout my entire college career but never put payments toward loans until I was out. So, debts kept stacking up. I tried to go into business with my father without establishing solid plans. I invested my time and he invested his money. Our misunderstanding of goals and direction had damaged our relationship for a long time. This was all due to lack of communication and planning at the start.

When I got my first job out of college, I quickly realized the degree I earned would only provide me with a job that could barely pay the bills. Not to mention the ability to start paying off my student loans. I worked for a nonprofit organization and it was the best job I could get. It was emotionally rewarding but not at all financially. I applied for loan forgiveness. Only problem is that it would have taken over 10 years of working a job that pays less than a living wage to do so. I wasn't going to wait that long because I financially couldn't. I was still living paycheck to paycheck and in way too much debt to keep earning so little. This career field sparked my passion to help others and to give back when I can. I love being able to be there for people that really need it. It's a shame these jobs don't pay enough to support the ones that are supporting so many in our communities.

After a couple years of doing this, I felt trapped in a spiraling debt-to-income differential. I had made many mistakes and it took a while but it was about time I learned from them. I started to look into finance books to see how I could help myself. To try and see what I was doing wrong but the only solution they ever provided was earn more and spend less. This should not be the only answer after over 400+ pages. I also started looking at the people in my life to see how they got where they were. After doing this, I sat down and started to take a good look at where I was financially and where I wanted to be. I've always had big dreams but lacked the focus and patience to achieve them. I started to focus on the things that I could change. It was time to adapt and overcome. I started to build my own path forward.

I changed careers and joined the military. This helped me get on my feet. This isn't the answer for everyone and not what I want you to get out of this book. However, it helped me find the discipline I needed and became financially stable. This allowed me to dabble in a few of the different ideas that I had been learning about and by merging some of them I created the process that I still use today. Some of the ideas I found were outdated or too outlandish. Some seemed more like gambling than investing. Then I finally came to a simple solution that focuses on an easy-to-follow plan that anyone could follow.

This plan got me to pay off my debts and start investing in retirement for the first time! Eventually, I was financially stable enough to buy my own home. I found that there needs to be an aggressive approach when it comes to money. I also found if you run before you can walk you will fall down. The aggressive approach I speak of isn't full of unnecessary risk. I say it needs to be an aggressive approach because that is the mentality that will keep you going. It will help you stick to your plan and to adjust when needed.

The plan is simple to follow and proven to work. It can be adjusted to fit any income and can be built as simply or as elaborate as you can handle. To start, keep it simple and slowly build onto the path as you see its progression. This information can be followed by anyone of any age. As always, the sooner you start the sooner your money will grow. So, let's get started!

1

Step One: Envisioning Your Kingdom

MOTIVATION

Everyone has different priorities and desires that drive them. What motives one person may not work for another but everyone has something that drives them. The key is to find out the ones that work best for you. I'm not talking about the little spark that helps for that one last pushup. This motivation is only good in the short term, not for going the distance. I'm talking about that marathon like motivation that keeps you going. The kind that fuels a fire in your heart at mile 23. Whether that is family, children, or the past you are running away from. For me it is the constant hunger to be better than I was yesterday! To have more money, travel to more places, and have the ability to give to those in need! I want to be able to surpass my own wildest dreams and inspire others to do the same. I want to create a chain reaction that impacts enough people to change a small portion of the world and in time have that influence continue to grow. Multiplying exponentially to the point where I look back with satisfaction knowing that I have made an impact. I found it best to set my goals higher than I think possible. That way if I come up short, at least I know I didn't settle for anything less than what I was capable of.

With all that said, let's start looking into what works for you. On a piece of scratch paper, write down some things that have motivated you in the past. How did it turn out? Did it work for a small task or work for an enduring project? Maybe it didn't work at all. These past experiences will help you identify what causes that fire to burn in you. This is a journey not a magic pill. You need to find what will drive you to stick with the plan and roll with the punches. This will allow you to adapt and overcome any obstacle that comes your way.

Many people are purely motivated by the end goal. If you know what your goals are this will be easier but if not then you will need to sit down and make another list. This list will consist of the things you want out of life. If you are married or have someone that you plan to live the rest of your life with it is important that you work on this together. This will set you up for better results and less arguing in the long run. What will make you feel fulfilled and satisfied with your achievement?

Make a list of the things you want to accomplish and then we can make a plan to start doing it!

This piece of scratch paper should act as your dream sheet. fill it up with things like the house you want to have, the car, the charitable donations, the retirement income you want and anything else that will make you happy and fulfilled in life. Then pick the one that drives you the most! If it's the house, find a picture of it and make it your bookmark. If it is the cash flow, use a dollar bill. If it is a charity, write that check you want to give in the future! (Don't sign it yet!) Whatever your drive is, make it into a bookmark so that you have a constant reminder of why you are doing this!

Another way to stay constantly motivated is to put pictures and reminders of your goals and dreams around your home. Such as on a bathroom mirror as some do when they are dieting. Put your plan and projection on the fridge so you see it everyday and continue to have the mindset that you can do this! This is the destination at the end of your path. Just as in any journey you need to start with two things to know your direction. Where you are now and where you want to go. We like to think of the future and see where we want to be but many people don't stop to see where they are now. That is the first mistake many people make on their journey and something that is essential to know as you start planning your journey.

Casey and Ashton's Goals

Casey and Ashton talked about their dream lives together and this is what they came up with.

1. Buy a house in the suburbs
2. Have two children
3. A college fund for each child
4. Pay off the house prior to retirement
5. Annual travel or big trips Bi-annually
6. Retire at or before the age of 60

IDENTIFY THE LIFE
YOU WANT

Now the path needs a destination. The dream of where you want to be and all the goals you wish to accomplish. You need to start with a clear end goal in sight so that you aren't throwing darts in the dark. Everything comes with a price tag and a timeline. You already made a list of some things that you desire. Now it's time to begin to estimate what that life will cost and how long it will take you to get there.

Go back to that list and feel free to add or subtract as you see fit. Put an estimated price tag on the things that are tangible. Things like a car, home, or business and add them up to start creating your retirement net worth goal. Anything intangible or unsellable such as an experience, a wedding, child, or travel will go on a separate list. Count these as savings funds but don't put them into your retirement net worth because they would have already happened prior to or aren't able to be sold. Another thing to account for is the amount of income from investments you wish to live off of during retirement.

For retirement income, come up with the amount you want as a monthly income. What would cover all your bills and allow you to live the way you want. Don't include social security in this because there is no guarantee it will be there for you. Then if you do get it, you can do even more of the things you want or give more to the ones you care about. When adding this up, think about where you want to live, this may change the amount needed to buy the same items. Another thing to keep in mind, will your home be paid off or will you be renting? There are many different variables that are involved with this so take your time and aim high so you don't have to live without.

The idea of financial independence is to live off the income that comes from your investments. Ideally you want to live off of 4% of your investments or less, this way it still grows and your monthly check will continue to increase. To explain the math, if I had a million-dollar retirement investment, 4% of that is $40,000 per year. Take that and divide it by 12 months and that is $3,333.33 per month. This would be your expected monthly income. To do this in reverse say you wanted to have $5,000 a month for retirement income. Multiply that by 12 months to get $60,000 per year. Divide that by 4% and you get a $1.5 Million-dollar retirement income investment goal.

Casey and Ashton's dream life cost

They currently rent and have $1000 in savings. By starting off with almost no assets they need to generate all of the net worth for their dream. The home they want is $300,000 and they want to purchase it in the next year or two. They also plan to start having kids during that same time frame. This will also start the clock on the college fund they want of at least $50000 for each child. Their ideal travel fund would be $4000 a year and to maintain their lifestyle in retirement they would need to make $5000 a month.

INFLATION

Now that we did all that dreaming and saw the big numbers, it's time to see how they add up. Your retirement investment goal and your tangibles should get added up as a net worth goal. The intangibles will be placed in a brokerage account or savings fund so that you can use them when the time comes. After you have your goals organized, quantified, and added up. It is important to add a multiple for inflation.

Let's say you want to have a million dollars for retirement based on today's prices. The likelihood of that million dollars still buying all the things you want in retirement is very low. Due to inflation, that million dollars will more than likely not have the same spending value that it did when you started saving. In the example below we show a simplified version of how $1 million changes for an average inflation of 2.5% per year for 25 years.

Example:

Year 1 $1,000,000.00 X 1.025 = $1,025,000.00

Year 2 $1,025,000.00 X 1.025 = $1,050,625.00

Year 3 $1,050,625.00 X 1.025 = $1,076,890.63

Year 4 $1,076,890.63 X 1.025 = $1,103,819.89

After 25 years, your new goal with inflation should actually be closer to $1,808,725.95. As you see, inflation can make a huge difference in the value of your money. It is impossible to predict the exact change in the value of a dollar but we can see trends from the past to help predict the future. The main idea is to continue to push the limits and set your goals high.

Casey and Ashton's New Financial goals

To figure this out they split their goals into three types of categories: net worth, funds, and short term. Their home and retirement income goes into their net worth category. They put their kids' college funds in the investment funds category and travel into a short-term savings section. To have a $5000 a month income they need to have a retirement income investment of around $1,500,000. Using the inflation projector on ToLiveLikeAKing.com to find the difference between what you want today and what you will need then. For Casey and Ashton this comes out to be $2,713,088.92 in 25 years. The house may gain value and add to your net worth as you pay down the mortgage. This addition to your net worth will not help in retirement income unless you consider the lack of a mortgage expense or you choose to sell the home in the future.

WORKING TOGETHER

As I continued on my journey, I met my wife and found the best way down this path is to work together as a team. That is what a family is a team. Sharing your financial life together can cause conflict from time to time. It also allows you to share goals and communicate what you want in life more fluently together. I can't emphasize enough how important it is to work with your spouse on your finances. You need to work together and figure out the end goal together or else someone will end up very disappointed. Working on your plan together will drastically increase the likelihood of you getting what you both want. This also gives you a partner in the process to help during times of struggle. By building and working on the plan together you avoid many arguments and gain an ally on the path to financial freedom. If you and your partner are on separate financial plans, it is like having two all-star players that don't pass the ball and are running different plays.

We personally have a joint checking and savings

that also feed each of our personal accounts with some "fun" money. This way if I want to save that fun money for something my wife thinks is stupid I can and if she wants something that I think is a waste she can. This makes us both happy and we have our joint accounts to do everything else.

This helps relieve some of the stress of your budget and allows you to buy gifts without each other realizing the money spent on it. Having joint accounts makes you both aware of how your finances are progressing and keeps everyone honest with their spending. Continue to go over your budget and spend time together monthly so that you can agree on how to proceed and celebrate your triumphs. This is only one of many ways to start working together but it's the one that I have seen the most success with.

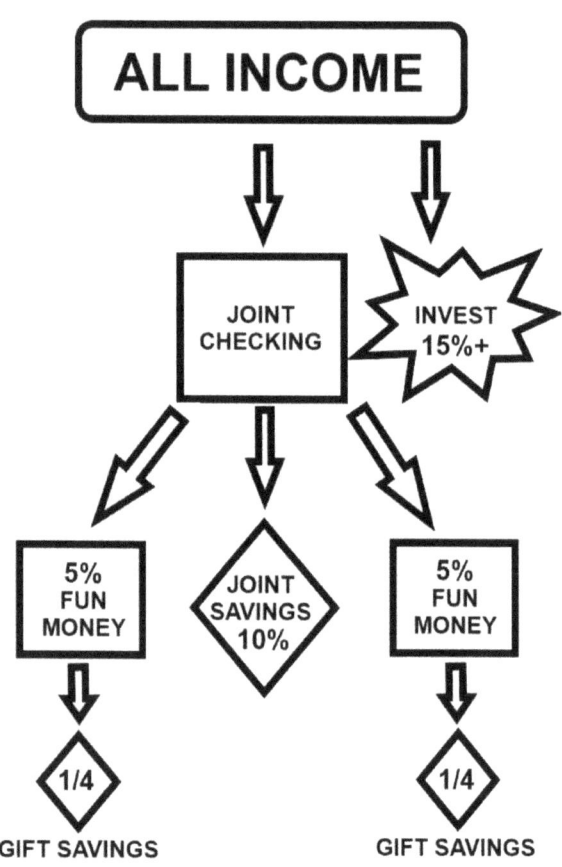

Cash Flow Example

2

Step Two: Knowing Where
You Are

A NEW BEGINNING

Now it's time to dig in and see where you stand. The first time doing this can be a very daunting task but each time gets faster to the point where it only takes minutes. Many people don't look into every purchase they make or try to figure out where all their money goes. That is exactly where you need to start! If you don't, it's like traveling through fog without a guiding light.

This is your personal ground zero, your new beginning. No more shall you wander in the fog. It is time for the light to guide you! So, let's get started tracking down where you are. To help you start off, go to ToLiveLikeAKing.com and download the free LLK Better Budgeting template. This will help you keep track of your path, aid in adding up your expenses, and predict investment growth. Next, you will need some more scratch paper to write down notes on each item as we go over them or go to the appendix and manually fill in the hard copy template.

INCOME

The first part is the fun part, your income. Write down your monthly income right off the pay slip. Whether it's from one source or multiple. Be sure to include all types if you get overtime, bonuses or tips. Then under each income stream put all the deductions and taxes that are taken from your pay. The excel sheet will take the difference of the income and all deductions to calculate your net income.

Now, let's calculate your monthly net income. For some people this is harder to predict. Most people don't get paid monthly so we will have to do some math and possibly some approximation in cases to get to your monthly income. Bi-monthly pay such as the 1st and 15th is easy; you just multiply it all by 2. If you are paid every other week multiply by 26 and then divide by 12. If you have variable income such as contract work or tips. It is best to take a years' worth of wages and divide by 12. If you don't have that number, take your best and worst months then average them out. This can be dangerous any time you are estimating so try to be conservative with your guess. This way any extra money is a blessing and not a curse if it ends up being less. The only income you shouldn't add to this is from investments. That will come in later. Below is a snapshot of the budgeting template.

CASEY	MONTHLY	ANNUALLY
SALARY:	$5,000.00	$60,000.00
Overtime:	$0.00	$0.00
Tips:	$0.00	$0.00
	$0.00	$0.00
TOTAL ENTITLEMENTS:	$5,000.00	$60,000.00
DEDUCTIONS:	MONTHLY	ANNUALLY
FED. INCOME TAX:	$600.00	$7,200.00
STATE INCOME TAX:	$175.00	$2,100.00
FICA - SOCIAL SECURITY:	$382.50	$4,590.00
FICA - MEDICARE:	$72.50	$870.00
TOTAL DEDUCTIONS:	-$1,230.00	-$14,760.00
NET INCOME:	$3,770.00	$45,240.00

Casey's Income Templet Example

Casey and Ashton's Income

Casey makes $60,000 a year salary; this breaks down to $5000 a month. Ashtons income is not so easy to break down the hourly wage plus tips can range from $700 a week to $1200 depending on the time of year. The average of this is $950 a week. $950x52=$49,400 a year or $4116.66 a month. The freelance work is very random but last year made a total of $10,000 but only $4,000 the year before. To average this out you get a monthly income of $583.33. This makes their household income $9,699 a month or $116,388 a year pretax and approximately to $7250 a month after taxes.

EXPENSES

This is the part that takes the most discipline. We are going to start by taking all of your expenses and split them into three categories: Housing, Food and Miscellaneous. This means going through every purchase and bill for the month. The idea here is not to make yourself look good as we naturally tend to do. You need to accurately document every expenditure. If you get upset by your spending habits this is good. It is more motivation to make a change. The idea is not to become a slave to your budget but to use it as a tool to free you. To allow you to do what you want at the same time as you achieve the goals that you have set out for.

By looking at all your purchases you will see how you spend your money and be able to apply this knowledge on future purchases. Maybe you didn't realize you spent over $100 at coffee shops. On the other hand, perhaps, this is one of the things you enjoy the most and see a way to adjust elsewhere. This should make you feel more at ease when you buy your $7 coffee because you know it's in the budget. The main idea here is to find out where you have any spending that is not essential to you. By eliminating non essential spending, you can make better use of this freed up cash flow. For now just document what you are currently doing by entering it in the expense report. Later on we'll go into how to adjust your spending. Here is Casey and Ashton's expenses. They worked on it together and now they see how they are spending their money.

HOME 20 - 30%	25%	$1,709.94
	MONTHLY	ANNUALLY
RENT	$1,800.00	$21,600.00
RENTERS INSURANCE	$130.00	$1,560.00
LAWN CARE	$100.00	$1,200.00
HOME TOTAL:	$2,030.00	$24,360.00
FOOD 10% OR LESS	10%	$683.98
	MONTHLY	ANNUALLY
GROCERIES AND TOILETRIES	$400.00	$4,800.00
DINNING OUT	$200.00	$2,400.00
FAST FOOD	$250.00	$3,000.00
LUNCHES	$200.00	$2,400.00
MEDICATIONS	$25.00	$300.00
FOOD TOTAL:	$1,075.00	$12,900.00
MISC. 20 - 35%	28%	$2,393.92
	MONTHLY	ANNUALLY
LIVING	MONTHLY	ANNUALLY
ELECTRIC	$100.00	$1,200.00
WATER	$75.00	$900.00
INTERNET	$129.00	$1,548.00
PHONE	$110.00	$1,320.00
TRASH	$75.00	$900.00
SECURITY SYSTEM	$45.00	$540.00
LIVING TOTAL:	$534.00	$6,408.00
TRANSPORTATION:	MONTHLY	ANNUALLY
VEHICLE PAYMENT:	$300.00	$3,600.00
VEHICLE PAYMENT:	$250.00	$3,000.00
REGISTRATION X2:	$15.00	$180.00
PARKING/TOLLS/GAS:	$250.00	$3,000.00
CAR WASHES	$50.00	$600.00
CAR INSURANCE	$220.00	$2,640.00
TRANSPORTATION TOTAL:	$1,085.00	$13,020.00
STREAMING	MONTHLY	ANNUALLY
TV	$89.00	$1,068.00
MUSIC	$15.00	$100.00
SHOWS	$35.00	$420.00
FITNESS	$45.00	$540.00
STREAMING TOTAL:	$184.00	$2,208.00
CHARITABLE GIVING	MONTHLY	ANNUALLY
CHARITY	$50.00	$600.00
CHARITABLE GIVING TOTAL:	$50.00	$600.00
PERSONAL	MONTHLY	ANNUALLY
PET MEDS	$15.00	$180.00
PET FOOD	$50.00	$250.00
PET GROOMING	$25.00	$300.00
PERSONAL HAIR	$50.00	$600.00
SPOUSE NAILS	$85.00	$1,020.00
SPOUSE HAIR	$200.00	$2,400.00
GYM	$300.00	$300.00
CLOTHES	$300.00	$3,600.00
OTHER	$550.00	$6,600.00
PERSONAL TOTAL:	$1,575.00	$18,900.00
MISC. TOTAL:	$3,428.00	
TOTAL EXPENSES:	$6,533.00	

NET WORTH

Now that we have gone over how to break down your monthly income and expenses. You should have a pretty good idea of where your cash flow is going. What does that add up to and what does it mean? This is why we calculate net worth. Your net worth is simply your total financial value. This is how you measure how well off an individual is and it is a simple calculation of all your liabilities subtracted from your total assets, savings and investments.

Let's start by going over your assets and liabilities to get a picture of your current net worth. Assets are anything of value that you could sell off if you needed too. This could be a house, car, collectables, jewelry, etc. For some of these things it may be easy to go online and get an estimated value and for others it may be more difficult. This is not the main focus unless you are actively trying to sell the item. For now, just make a list of estimated values of the more difficult items. If you have the urge to dive in deeper you can do so at a later time.

Liabilities are any kind of debt that you have such as student loans, personal loans, a mortgage, car loan, credit card debt, etc. To keep easy track of these debts, make a list and include the value of the object, your home or car. If its school loans or credit cards are zero since you can't sell them. Then put the amount owed, the percent interest and finally the minimum payment. This will be very helpful when we talk about how to pay off this debt. Take a look at the example below to see how to enter it into the templet. After completing both of these lists it will be time to dive into any of the savings and investments you may have.

DEBTS	VALUED AT	AMOUNT OWED	INTEREST	MONTHLY PAYMENT
CAR	$15,000.00	$23,000.00	3.500%	$300.00
CAR	$8,000.00	$10,000.00	7.000%	$225.00
CREDIT CARD	$0.00	$3,500.00	25.000%	$45.00
TOTAL	$23,000.00	$38,000.00	DIFFERENCE	-$15,000.00

OTHER ASSETS	VALUE
ELECTRONICS	$1,000.00
JEWELRY	$2,000.00
OTHER	$0.00
TOTAL	$3,000.00

Casey and Ashton's Current Assets and Liabilities

Savings and investments are the strength of your net worth and overall financial well being. We will go over the ideal amount and type for all of these accounts as we continue on our path but for now list out all the ones you have. When entering these accounts list out the value, type, and location. This will help you keep track of each account as you go. This is also good in the event that anything should happen to you. Your family will be able to find things much easier. This is how Casey and Ashton have saved and invested so far. As you can see they have a long way to go to get to their goals.

SAVINGS 10%			MONTHLY	ANNUAL				
			$731.35	$8,776.25				
PRIORITY	TYPE OF FUND	MONTHLY INPUT	CURRENT FUNDS	ACCOUNT NAME	FULLY FUNDED	MONTHS UNTIL FUNDED	YEARS UNTIL FUNDED
1	EMERGENCY	$600.00	$1,000.00	SAVINGS	$10,000.00	15	1.25
2	TRAVEL	$100.00	$150.00	SAVINGS	$6,000.00	58.5	4.88
3	HOUSE	$600.00	$0.00	SAVINGS	$15,000.00	25.0	2.08
	TOTALS	$1,300.00	$1,150.00	ALL:	$31,000.00		

INVESTMENTS 15% (FIRE 40%+)			15%	40%	
			$1,097.03	$2,925.42	
PRIORITY	TYPE OF FUND	MONTHLY INPUT	CURRENT FUNDS	ACCOUNT NAME	
1	CASEY 401 K	$400.00	$1.00	CASEY 401 K	
2	529	$200.00	$0.00	COLLEGE	
#REFI	ASHTON IRA	$400.00	$0.00	ASHTON IRA	
	TOTALS	$1,000.00	$1.00		

**Casey and Ashton's Current Savings
and Investments**

Now that you did all the leg work, it's time to see exactly where you are financially. As it was stated before, now you will find your net worth by adding up all your assets, savings, and investments then subtracting your total debts. If you have filled in the template properly it will have already done this for you.

Savings	$	1,000.00
Investments	$	5,000.00
Assets	$	26,000.00
Debts	$	(38,000.00)
CURRENT NET WORTH =	$	(6,000.00)

Casey and Ashton's Current Net Worth

As you see in Casey and Ashton's example above, it is very easy to have a negative net worth if you owe money to different lenders or don't save and invest. Now that you see where you stand it is time to move forward. To pave your path and strive to earn your throne!

With the information you have entered into the budgeting template you have your current net worth. The next tab will help you project how it can grow through your investments. When you look at your results and projections you may be very disappointed after seeing how much you need to change to create your dream or you may already be on track. Either way, now you know where you stand and why you need to take action. Finding out what it takes will depend on many factors. Your path will be as unique as where you currently are and where you want to be.

The best way to keep you motivated is to set checkpoints along the way. As you lay out your path, go back through your intermediate goals and put a timeline to them. This will give you many little finish lines to go after on the way to your end goal of financial independence. As I started down my path, I made easy check points that made a big difference and kept motivating me to strive for the next. My goals were things like start to invest, save $1000, stick to the budget for one month and stick to the budget for one year.

In the next section, we will go over ways to make the necessary changes to get where you want and pave your path. You will see how making some simple adjustments can make a large difference in a short amount of time and a massive difference down the road. Sticking to the path is the key to it all. To do this look at those motivators to take action to earn your throne and continue to reach for your crown!

3

Step Three: Paving Your Path

ADAPT AND OVERCOME

After seeing where you stand, it is time to start looking at your own personal finances as a business. The business mindset's only biased to what is profitable and doing everything you can to avoid being in the red. It's time to adapt and overcome. With this mentality, it is easier to make decisions because it is simply based on whether it will be a good investment or not. Does it help or hurt my potential to reach my goals? I'm not saying to live a life where you don't do anything fun but to know when enough is enough.

Adapt and overcome is a common phrase that has a lot of emotion behind it. People have many hardships that we overcome and it's important to use these feelings to push you. It won't all be easy! Sticking to a plan is easier said than done. It is important to keep the end in sight so you know where you are going, why you are doing it, and focus on staying on track.

The way you adapt and overcome is by starting with understanding two main concepts; lifestyle creep and living below your means. Knowing this can make a huge impact right away without needing to work harder to increase your income or losing all that well deserved free time. With an understanding of these two concepts, you will start to see how you got where you are and how easy it is to get pushed off track. It is your job to recognize this and get back on the path to our dream.

Lifestyle creep is usually a slow process. It is when someone starts to increase their income and as they do that, they start to increase their expenses. An over simplified example of this would be; now that you got a promotion or a raise you stop packing your lunch and start to get it delivered to you on your break. This significantly increases your daily expenses and makes it so your entire raise or even more is spent on something you never did before. By doing this, you lost that raise and are in the same place as you left off financially or worse just for a fancy lunch. I'm not saying to never treat yourself but you had no problem packing that lunch before. This is one example of how people lose what they earned almost as soon as they get it. Other examples are buying a new car with a larger payment or upgrading their monthly subscriptions. All of these things are easy to do but they suck out your money every month like a leach. After you are further down the path these things will be well in your reach. Don't give up your raise while you are just starting down the path to financial freedom.

Living below your means can be taken many different ways. The kind I'm talking about is living without a lot of excess. In our society it seems that we have a tendency to over indulge and live way beyond our actual means. We should be spending less than you earn instead of more. It's not living like you're starving or never doing anything fun and pinching every penny. It's just planning things out and not spending to the point of excess. You could go out to eat less often and make more meals at home. Another example I enjoy is substituting a more expensive activity with a free one that is just as fun. Instead of hanging out at the mall where you are going to spend money. Head to the park or a beach.

Living below your means is the best way to free up cash flow for saving and investing in that future dream that you are working hard for. This doesn't mean only eating rice and beans. It simply means not going out and spending every cent just because you can. Prioritize the things that make you happy and focus on them. Living below your means may be living closer to work or driving a more cost-effective car. Whatever it is, make it work for you. It is your kingdom to rule and your dream to realize. The rate that you get there depends on how you prioritize it.

Simple changes like these can help you spend less than you earn and free you from the paycheck-to-paycheck lifestyle. By following these examples, you can save thousands every year. Now that savings can be invested and will significantly help you on the financial journey to your dream life. With these two concepts in mind, you can start to adjust your expenses. Focus on doing the things you want to do while living below your means and reducing any lifestyle creep.

INCOME DISTRIBUTION

Beginning with the basics of budgeting is a great way to start. Budgeting is thought by most as a restrictive activity but as discussed in step two, we all have a budget. You just might not be keeping track of yours. The real question is do your finances control you or do you control your finances? Are you a slave to your money or are you using it to free yourself? Even if you haven't been budgeting in the past. You see now that the aftermath of your spending activity is just an uncontrolled budget. It's time for you to get in control of your cash flow to get the outcomes that you are planning for.

Now that you know how you are spending your money and your net worth. Let's look into the common standard for cash flow vs. a more aggressive income distribution to see how your budget and goals lineup. In the following table you will see the spending and savings plan that is commonly preached and below it is the Financial

Independence Retire Early (FIRE) income distribution.

AFTER TAX INCOME:	MONTHLY $7,313.54	ANNUALLY $87,762.48
STANDARD SAVE FOR RETIREMENT		
HOUSING	30%	$2,194.06
FOOD	10%	$731.35
SAVINGS	10%	$731.35
INVESTMENT	15%	$1,097.03
MISC.	35%	$2,559.74
FINANCIAL INDEPENDENCE RETIRE EARLY		
HOUSING	20%	$1,462.71
FOOD	10%	$731.35
SAVINGS	10%	$731.35
INVESTMENT	40%	$2,925.42
MISC.	20%	$1,462.71

Casey and Ashton's Income Distribution
Comparison

The FIRE type distribution is focused heavily on investing and saving to retire as early as possible. The idea is for you to live off of the income from investments to enjoy retirement as early and as long as you possibly can. This large input will help your investments accounts grow rapidly via your income as well as market growth. Once you have the amount necessary to live off the investment income, you would be able to retire if you choose to. This concept isn't for everyone for several reasons. One of them is that the income they are trying to live off may not support the retirement they had dreamt about. Another reason that many people get bored in retirement and will end up going back to the workforce. On the other side of the coin, most financial advice will tell you to save 10% and invest 15% of your income to be financially successful. However, this generic advice has led many to less than the life that they had hoped for and worked well into their glory days because of it.

The best thing to do is to edge your finances closer to the FIRE distribution when possible or work to that goal. This doesn't mean you have to retire early. It simply sets you up financially quicker. This also allows you to decide what is best for you instead of your finances deciding it for you. In order to do this we need to increase our incomes, decrease our spending and boost our investments. This is the battle of average vs the ideal but the verdict is still out and it's all up to you!

BUILDING YOUR BUDGET

In step two, you wrote out all your monthly expenses, entered all your income, assets, and liabilities in your budget template. By doing this you already made your current budget. Now it's time to adjust it. There are many ways to go through this process and everyone will have their own preference.

You can dive right in and make changes right now. To see what works for you. Then try to do it for a month or two to see if you can live that way. This is called the make or break method. It can be instantly rewarding but if unsuccessful it is a massive blow to future motivation. You could start out small to see how your expenses will change now that you are paying more attention to them. You may even do a bit of both. Just remember to stick to the plan you set. Move at your own pace. Make it feel more freeing than restrictive. You will be more comfortable and successful by doing so. Also, just because you put an amount in a column on your budget doesn't mean you have to spend up to that amount. You could always pocket the rest in savings or use it on something else.

The Goal is to try and make your expense distribution look as follows. For your home spending it is recommended to use 30-20% or less of your net income. This includes your rent or mortgage and any insurance, services or fees that are a part of it. When it comes to food, spending 10% or less is recommended. This is all your groceries and going out altogether. Lastly is your miscellaneous spending. These are all the things that aren't needed to live. If it isn't food, water or shelter. It is miscellaneous. Good thing this is the largest section of your expenses at 35-20% or less.

The idea is to live below your means but be comfortable. Get as much of your income past the expenses portion so that you have what you need to make your dream happen. The rest of your income is for paying off debt, increasing savings and investing in the dream. This should make up 25-50% or more of your income based off of whatever made it through the gauntlet of expenses. This is the goal for your path. As you get closer to the 50% or more mark, you're going to see vast improvement and massive benefits in the long run.

Some easy ways to decrease expenses can be found everywhere on the internet and it all goes back to living below your means. Here are some more examples that I have personally used and found very helpful. You can save on gas by car-pooling or combining trips so that you use less. This saves time and money. Buying groceries every two weeks makes you think more about what you need to buy by planning meals out. Stock up on things that you use more often. This leads to less food wasted and less trips to the store. Use your freezer to prevent food turning rancid. Eat your food before the expiration date to prevent food waste. Besides the fact that there are so many people without food and wasting it isn't helping that. By wasting food, you essentially are paying double for that meal. You paid for the meal that went bad and the one you ate instead. Lastly, find ways to have fun that don't cost a lot or are free to do. Riding a bike, hiking, hanging out with friends on the beach and walks in the park are just a few low-cost things that are fun and promote a healthy lifestyle.

Automating your finances is a great way to save time and stick to the plan. Time is more valuable than anything else because it's the one thing you can't buy more of. By periodically checking and managing your accounts you can verify everything is going as planned and save time doing so. It is best to do this bi-weekly or at least monthly. The more bills and investments you can automate the easier it will be to reach all your goals and the more free time you will have to do the things you love. I suggest having as much of your cash flow automated as possible this way all you need to do is supervise and minor changes.

You paved the path with your budget and found out where you could save money. This is now allowing you to distribute more money to your savings, eliminate debt, and add to your investments. Our next step involves increasing income, saving for future events, and eliminating your bad debts. This is how you earn your throne!

Automated Finances

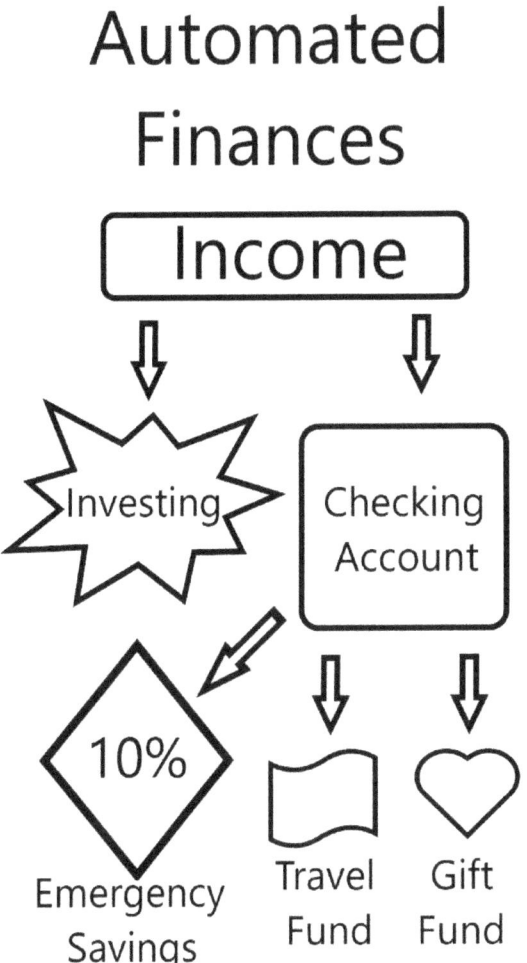

Automated Finances Flow Chart

4

Step Four: Earning Your Throne

INCREASING YOUR INCOME

Boosting your income can come in many shapes and forms. The most common is getting a better paying job or a raise. You could also increase your expendable income by eliminating expenses. Doing this will make your current income go further. Side hustles work great but remember not to lose a work life balance by doing so. The whole point of having wealth is to enjoy life and help others to do the same. If you are always working you are doing neither. Many people try to use every minute to improve their income without realizing they are living to work not working to live.

So how do you increase your income without spending all your time working? This is where synergizing comes into play. Trying to find things that you already do that could be turned into something profitable. If you have hobbies that produce things like furniture or art. You can make money from a hobby like Ashton does freelancing as a painter then your work will be one of the things you most enjoy. Selling these things would add to your income without taking you away from the things you enjoy doing. Maybe your current work produces a byproduct that is simply being disposed of instead of sold or turned into another product. By doing this you are making more with the same amount of time at work. Just make sure you have permission to use anything that is getting thrown out. By asking before you do this you will save a lot of possible legal issues. If your employer says no, try asking if you could do it for the company. This shows initiative and may end up giving you a better paying position at the company.

Another option is finding ways to make passive income. Similar to how your investments make money with little to no effort on your behalf. There are many other ways to make money with little to no effort after the initial set up. For instance, many people put advertisements on their streaming channels or advertise products on their web sites, so that they can make money off of affiliate marketing. Song writers, actors, and book authors all make a profit off the sale of their products. The initial effort is great but the sales provide passive income afterward.

Just remember, increasing your income doesn't help if you don't save it or put it into investments. Lifestyle creep can be hard to avoid. Increasing income is not how you gain wealth. Producing income from your assets and investments is how you increase wealth. Make your money work for you. Don't let it leave your pockets as fast as it found its way there.

SAVINGS

Savings is not an investment, it is an emergency stash of cash. Even if you make 1-2% on interest from the bank. It is likely to be less than the increase due to inflation. Inflation fluctuates from less than a percent to over 5%. This means you may actually be losing money not "Saving" it. A good goal for your personal emergency fund, as most financial advisers would suggest, is 3 to 6 months expenses. This will help you continue to live your normal life if something unexpectedly pops up like a loss of job or any other significant financial situation.

The amount to save will vary depending on your life situation. If you have a very volatile career, it may be better to save more. If you are single or have a single income household it makes more sense to lean toward 6 months expenses. If your career is extremely stable or has multiple income sources, it is easier to get away with closer to 3 months expenses. If you have an older car or rental property you should have a separate emergency fund for these things as well. For these funds I would find the price to fix or replace the most expensive issues. Use a new car engine, HVAC for the house or a new roof as a goal amount for these funds.

To start out aim smaller and then work your way up to it. Remember, you should have between 25 to 50% or more of monthly income remaining for savings, debt elimination, and investing. After paying the minimum payment on all your debts, put the remainder in savings until you reach a starter goal of $1500 to $2000. After you reach this, make the adjustment to use 10% of your income to continue the growth in your savings. Use the rest to eliminate debt and invest in your future. This way you can start maximizing gains without the risk of not being able to pay for any kind of unexpected bills.

Other savings funds are important too. The holidays and anniversaries come at the same time every year but people go into crazy amounts of debt over them. People travel all over for different reasons every year and never save up for it. They just swipe a card and accrue debt over something that shouldn't have been a surprise. It is important to have a separate savings account for these things. Presents and travel are not emergencies. You should be expecting these expenses and saving up for them. Anything that is an expected annual expense or will happen in less than 2-3 years is best put in a savings account instead of investing. This is due to the high risk involved in short term investments.

Casey and Ashton's savings plan

After shuffling around their expenses and agreeing on a budget. They made it possible to put 10% in their emergency savings each month. They started a travel fund savings account with direct deposits of $200 a month. They also have $1300 or 18% of their income to start eliminating their debt. By making these adjustments, they are now saving roughly 30% of their monthly income.

DEBT ELIMINATION

Now let's start to go over what to do with the rest of that 25 to 50% or more. Debt can creep up on you in many forms. Credit cards can be convenient ways to make purchases. With all the perks and rewards it can be very enticing to get them. If you can control yourself and pay them off in full every month, the rewards can be very nice. However, some people treat them as free money instead of debt that can cripple their potential wealth generation. If you don't pay off the balance on a card that has 25% APR you accrue that much more debt every month. 25% APR or Annual percentage rate is 2.08% every month so that 1.5% in rewards cash you "earned" won't even cover the APR. If you always pay them off and you continue to only buy the things that you would as if you had cash in hand, only then would you be actually earning 1.5% in returns. But let's get real, 1.5% isn't anything to brag about. If you are using this excuse to charge it, think of another one. Don't get me wrong I use these cards too but most for different perks like lounge access or free subscriptions and I pay them off in full every month.

Credit cards however are not the only debt to talk about. Many people have a mortgage, car loan, student loan, personal loans, and so many more. Today is the day, you look down at all the creditors and say "You aren't stealing my dream life!" In step two we made a list of all our debts including the total amounts and interest rates. Now you are going to organize these by interest rate and create your debt avalanche. Debt snowballs are fine too but they aren't as effective. A debt avalanche is when you pay off debts with the highest interest rate first. This rapidly stops the build up of debt from the monthly interest. Then move the money from that payment to the next debt. A snowball is when you pay off the smallest total debt amount owed first to build confidence and move that money to the next debt. In step one we went over motivation and if the snow ball fits for you then go for it. This way will take longer and more money to pay off your debt.

Now that we understand the difference in approaches, we should also look at the concept of bad vs not as bad debt. For instance, any debt that is less than the market average percent growth should be considered not as bad debt. This general rule indicates that interest rates higher than what is expected to be made in the market is bad debt. For example, if the average investment will make 7%,a conservative look on the average S&P 500 growth. Then a debt is "bad debt" if it is equal to or greater than 7%. Instead of putting extra money in investments, you should pay off bad debt since the gains from your investment won't be greater than the interest on your debt. This also means that good or not as bad debt is 6% or less. These debts tend to be low interest loans such as your mortgage or some car loans. Putting extra cash towards these debts may not benefit you as much as investing.

So set up your avalanche by putting all your extra cash left over from expenses minus 15% for savings and investments. This will be for starting that emergency fund and matching any employer investments if available while paying off your debts. That's right, even if you have bad debt, if your employer has a match for your retirement then the investment will be better than paying off debt. This is due to the instant 100% increase every time they match your input. Debt elimination is a crucial part of the path. This is what stops the leaches from sucking your dream away from you.

First, remember to pay all the minimums on your debts to keep them current. Every extra dollar gets added to the minimum for the debt with the highest interest. As each of your debts get paid off, take all the cash going to that debt's payment and add it to the next highest interest debt. Continue to do this until all you have is low interest debt. At that point it is up to you to decide to keep paying off debt or move it all to savings and investments. Just remember, the key to having your investments work for you. Starting as early as possible is the way you can make gains on top of your gains through compounding interest. Compounding interest is simply the interest gained from the reinvestment of the previous years. This is how your money will grow exponentially.

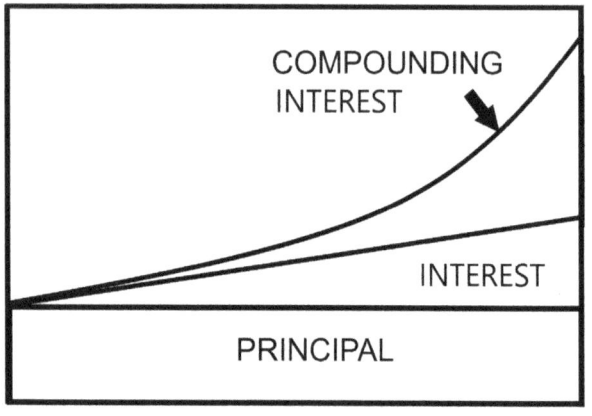

Compounding Interest Visual

5

Step Five: Reaching for the Crown

HAVING THE END
IN SIGHT

As you make your way down this path, you'll see it's not going to change overnight but your attitude toward it can. Some things will change immediately and some will take much longer. Don't lose that motivation from step one. Make things easier on yourself and always keep the end in mind.

Make as many of your payments, savings and investments automatic deposits. By doing this, you don't have to think about all the steps and you still get where you want to go. Just like walking, you don't think about each step. You focus on where you are headed. Automating investments prior to hitting your bank is one of the best things you can do. If you don't see the money, it is never missed. Instead, it goes straight to growing in your investments and building your future.

Sticking to your plan is essential to the success of your financial journey. Many obstacles will try to get in your way. By keeping the motivation to adapt and overcome obstacles, you will win every time. Keep pushing toward your end goals. Don't forget all the motivational reminders you have around the house. The best way to stick to the plan is to be able to see the finish line.

Everyone in a race puts on the afterburners when they see that finish line, trying to get there as soon as possible. They had the energy to try harder the entire race but they weren't motivated to unleash it until they saw the final stretch. In order to help with this for your finances, look at the final tab in the LLK Better Budgeting Template. This is to help predict where you will end up based on what you are doing today. If you don't like what you see, make the changes you need to so that you can reach that end goal you desire. This is your personal finish line, your crown, and it's in reach.

Through investing, saving and staying out of debt. You can make massive changes in the outcome of your life and legacy. In this section, we will go over the simple plan for investing as well as some more information on other options. As I said before, I have dabbled in many ways of investing. One way can work for everyone but there are many ways to adjust it to what is best for you. You never want to stop learning. Keep looking for more information and use this search for knowledge to help motivate you to continue to reach for your crown.

Casey and Ashton's projections

Once they have their bad debts settled, they plan on moving that money to a brokerage account for their dream home and college funds for their children. They will also be putting $600 a month into Casey's 401K. In 20 years, Casey will be able to stop working after earning a pension. A pension plan that pays out 50% of your average pay of $60,000 is a lifetime of $1,812.50 monthly payments. 5 years of $500 in a brokerage account with 7% return adds up to $26,639.66 for a down payment on their first home together. After paying for the down payment, they will move the $500 a month to an IRA in Ashton's name. $200 a month will go to the children's college fund and that adds up to over $107,000 in 20 years with 7% returns.

Making these changes has drastically changed the outlook of their future and has paved the path so they can reach all their goals. Casey and Ashton will have a travel fund for annual vacations. They will be able to buy their home. The children will have over $50,000 each for college. They will both be able to retire at or before the age of 60 with the income they desired. This is their dream life. After planning and doing the hard work, they got everything they wanted and more. Not to mention, they would have a million-dollar net worth by the age of 55.

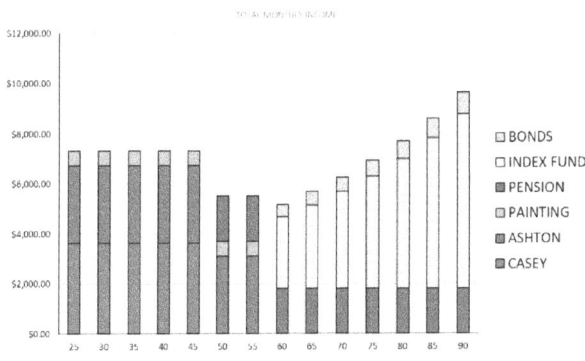

Casey and Ashton's Projected Monthly Income

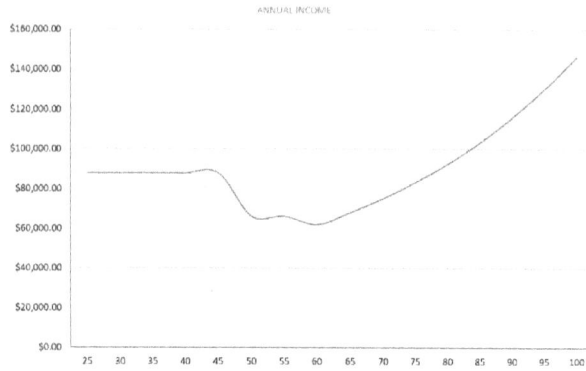

**Casey and Ashton's Projected Annual
Income**

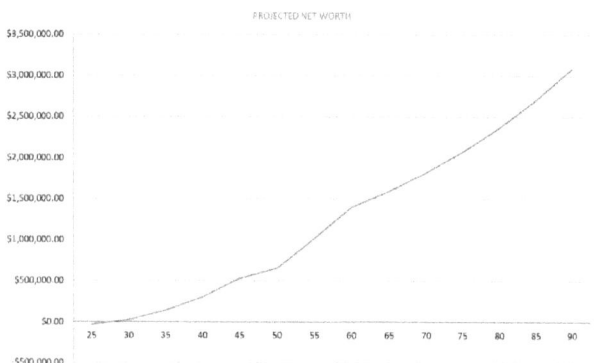

**Casey and Ashton's Projected Net
Worth**

INVESTING IN YOUR FUTURE

What is financial freedom? For those who do not know, this is when you can live off your investments and not have to work to continue your current way of life. In order to do this, we need to have enough in our investments to support an income to live the way we want to. For a simple example, let's say you live in a different economy and have $100 invested. Through your investments, you earn $7 that year. In this magical economy, you can live off less than that $7 per year. This would be considered independently wealthy. This financial freedom, it is what you are building up to with your plan in today's economy. This way you are not digging into that nest egg.

To start, let's go over some of the best practices for your path to come. Then we'll go into some basic details on other options so that you can see the differences. You will also see why some options are safer than others and how they historically tend to add up.

THE KEY TO YOUR DREAM

To review, you should have 25-50% or more to use in savings, debt elimination and investing. Now let's say your debt avalanche is complete and you only have the low interest debts. The low interest debt like your mortgage and maybe your car payment should be already in your expenses. Don't add that into your 25-50% or more. 10% of this should continue to go in your savings until you reach your goals and that leaves 15-40% or more going into your investments.

This first bit of advice was already hinted on. An example is any kind of employer retirement fund, like a 401K or Thrift Savings Plan. If they do an employer match, you are losing money by not getting the match if they provide one. This is as close to free money as it gets! The next key thing is to see if they have a Roth IRA. In a Roth you will be investing after-tax dollars. This means it was taxed prior to investing opposed to adding it as income tax when you take it out. This has two main benefits. The first, is that your account value on your statement is the actual value you will be able to take out. Secondly, after following your path to financial independence you should be making more money in retirement than you are now so it should get taxed less than it would have in a traditional IRA.

The maximum investment in these accounts changes frequently so it is good to look them up annually. Striving to max out the annual deposits in these accounts should be one of your major investment goals. The next depends on if you want to retire before the age of 59 and a half or not. If you want to retire at that time, the next thing to do after maxing out your employer investment plan would be to open up your own IRA account. Invest in this up to the max. If your spouse works, they can do the same. If you are blessed enough to max out all of these accounts you can open up an individual brokerage account. This type of account has no limits on the amount you can deposit but doesn't have the same tax benefits as a retirement account. If you want to retire prior to 59 and a half you should be investing in an individual brokerage account as well as a retirement account. That way you can live off the brokerage account until you are able to withdraw from your retirement account without penalties.

Another reason to have an individual broker-age account is to have long term savings for those events down the road. This is a great place to put a wedding or baby fund. As you save for these things, they can be invested and grow until you need it. Just remember if you are saving for less than a few years it would be safer to put this money in a high yield savings account because the market is too unpredictable in the short term. Inside these retirement and brokerage accounts, there are different types of ways to invest as well.

You should have all of these types of accounts in companies that don't charge excessive fees or restrictions that prevent you from investing. Many companies try to charge fees that is why it is best to do your research prior to opening an account. The accounts themselves should be invested in a total market index fund such as Vanguard's VT-SAX / VOO, Fidelities FZROX or Charles Schwab SWTSX. These total market index funds tend to mirror the S&P 500. This is a dependable way to increase returns without excessive risk. The S&P

500 has averaged just over 10% from 1972 to 2022 and there isn't any reason to believe that this will change. I don't suggest that you plan on having them increase by 10% for planning purposes. I would use something much more conservative like 7%. This way you aren't disappointed if the market doesn't go the way it has for 50 years or you end up retiring while the market is down. Later on, we will go over mutual funds and other investment options that are reliable low-cost investments without unnecessary risk.

Once you have the invested amount that you calculated in your dream plan. It is time to start making your future investments more resilient to risk by investing a portion in bonds and CDs. This is something that won't make as much money but it will grow to match inflation and there is almost no risk. A good time to do this is about 8 years before your retirement date or after you hit your magic number. Whichever happens first is best. Split up your current investments by putting a safety net in bonds or CDs and the rest to continue to grow with the market. When you do this, make sure you can still live off your investment income because the return on CDs and bonds is much less than index funds. Some suggest 60% index and 40% CD/bonds but this will depend on your age and how risk averse you are. By splitting up your investments, you can have a dependable safety blanket to weather any storm that hits the market.

If your job is one of the few that has a pension plan, it is best to try to ride it out to at least the minimum obligated term to be eligible. This way you can live off the pension income and all the investments become extra income rather than your only income. I suggest if you do plan on retiring early, have a side hustle that you love to do. If you don't want one and can live off the investments that great but this can provide some extra income. It is also a great way to avoid boredom and provide purpose. Many hobbies can fit right into a side hustle. You will love what you are doing and enjoy spending time doing it. At this point you should have reached every goal you had set and life you have been dreaming of. The plan is to not depend on social security but to rely on yourself. If it's not there you won't be going hungry and if it is there you can raise your quality of life as you see fit.

This is the path that has changed my financial

life and continues to set my family up for the long haul. Keep on your path and if you ever veer off track you know how to get back on it. Get your mind set on the future. Use what motivates you to push you through the hard times and all the way to your finish line. Automate as much as possible. Live below your means and push off the lifestyle creep. Focus on eliminating debt and invest like it's going out of style. Follow your path and you will make it to your destination. The last step will introduce more information on different types of investments and insurance. It is important to never stop learning. The more you seek out information on wealth and finances the more you will keep your path in mind and that is the most useful tool to stay motivated. Knowledge is the one thing that no one can take away from you. The more you discover the better off you will be. Now, let's expand your empire!

6

Step Six: Expanding Your Empire

MARKET INDEX, ETF, AND MUTUAL FUNDS

Index funds are not managed by any individual accountant but committees that group companies that meet their specifications. These funds can be traded like stocks but perform more consistently than individual stocks. This diversification alleviates some of the risks involved in stock trading. Index funds are traded at the beginning and end of the trading day but Some ETFs are made to mirror these funds. ETFs can be traded during all market hours. The main US markets are the S&P 500, NASDAQ, Russell 200, and Dow Jones.

Index investments are more predictable because of the long-term data available and infrequent change in structure. They are very easy to use for any beginner investor and tend to be lower risk than mutual funds or individual stocks. Mutual funds tend to have management fees to pay for the financial broker managing the account. They are called mutual funds based on the idea that it is a group of people pitching in to buy groups of stocks picked by the broker.

Mutual funds and ETFs that are not index based are harder to predict due to the flexibility in structure of the investments made by the broker or group and the lack of long-term data. They may outperform the market one year and not the next. There are many different types of funds. However, it takes greater knowledge than the average investor to know the pros and cons of each mutual fund or ETF.

STOCKS:
GROWTH AND DIVIDEND

Investing in a "Growth" stock is simply investing in a company's stock with the hopes that the overall value will increase. They may or may not also pay out dividends but the main focus is the company's growth in value. When investing in any individual stock, it is not a good idea to put all your eggs in one basket. If that company goes bankrupt, so do you. It is best to diversify your portfolio if you are picking stocks and to invest for the long term. Picking companies for short stints such as seasonal or day trading is closer to gambling than investing.

Investing in a shaky economy can always be nerve racking. Dividend stocks are the safer way to go if you don't feel comfortable in growth stocks but still want to dabble in stocks. They tend to be with more stable companies, especially the ones that are selling goods and commodities. The stock prices are more stable and the income from dividends are steady. Look into the dividend payout history of these stocks. You can see when they pay out and how consistent they have been in the past. Each company is different and some have paused dividend payouts in the past. Payouts for most companies are quarterly but some payout monthly. The best option for consistent payouts without putting all your eggs in one basket is to find multiple companies that have different dividend distribution months. This can make it so you have quarterly companies but get paid or reinvest every month. Dividend yield is the percentage paid out per share of stock that is owned during the period. For instance, if the stock has a dividend yield of 3% at a price of $50 each then your payout will be as follows.

A $250 investment at $50 per share x 3% = $1.50 per share x 5 shares = $7.50 a year or $1.875 a quarter or $.0625 every month.

A $100,000 investment at $50 per share x 3% = $1.50 per share x 2000 shares = $3000 a year or $750 a quarter or $187.50 every month.

As you can see, there isn't much income from a smaller investment. However, on a larger scale investment or higher dividend yield can make a lot of passive income. If you have four of these investments on different quarterly distribution cycles you would receive a quarterly dividend every month. If you don't need the income because you are already living below your means and saving for the future, then reinvest the dividends and your payouts will continue to grow. By the time you retire this could end up being quite a substantial supplemental income. You also won't have to wait until 59 and a half to reap the benefits.

CDS AND BONDS

These are considered to be two of the safest types of investments but they historically yield less than an index but it is better than most savings account for long term safe money. CDs or certificates of deposit are for all intents and purposes like a loan that you are giving to the bank. There is a set duration of time that is attached to the investment. Once it has matured you will have made interest from the loan you gave to the bank. This interest rate will vary which puts you in competition with inflation. The main idea is to make the value of your money in these investments be greater than or stay equal to the rate of inflation. The goal is to have the CD outpace inflation.

A bond is similar to a CD, they are both like loans. They both have a set amount of time needed to mature. Except a bond is a loan to the government or a company that is issuing them. A bond will have a set interest rate that will change by the length of term and agency providing the bond. They will maintain value as long as the company or government doesn't go bankrupt or collapse. A U.S. government bond is about as safe as it gets.

The Strategy to start investing in CDs or Bonds is to split your investment into five equal parts. Invest each portion into its own term so that one of them matures each year. That would make it a one-, two- three-, four- and five-year term. The longer the term the higher the return rates given. This also incurs some risk since you will get charged a fee if you take it out prior to maturity. After the first one matures, take any profit needed for income out and reinvest the rest in another 5-year term. Doing this every year will eventually have it so you have a 5-year CD or bond maturing every year.

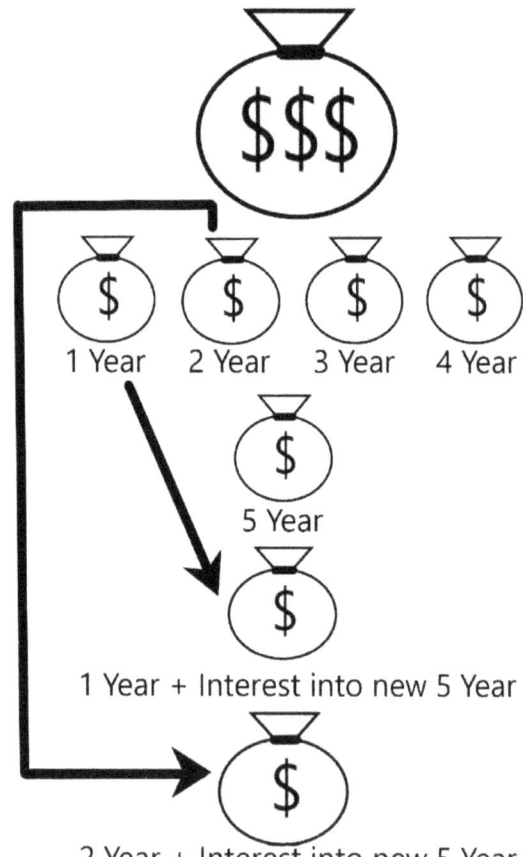

1 Year 2 Year 3 Year 4 Year

5 Year

1 Year + Interest into new 5 Year

2 Year + Interest into new 5 Year

Bond / CD Investment Strategy

PENSIONS AND ANNUITIES

Pensions are given by certain employers as a way of paying for the loyalty of their employees. They do this by guaranteeing that they will pay a set amount to their employees for the rest of their lives. The only condition is that they work for them for a preset time frame. For a government pension such as military, post office, teaching, etc. this is usually a 20-year commitment. At the completion of that term, you start getting payments issued to you for the rest of your life, without needing to work any additional time. These payments are a percentage of the amount you were getting paid prior to retirement. In some cases, after earning one pension, people can work for another company to earn a second.

A similar idea is an annuity. However, this is not from your employer, this is more like buying retirement insurance. An annuity can be something you make payments on until it hits a maturity amount or something you pay for in a lump sum. It can start immediately after payment or at a later date. It all depends on the issuer and the contract you agree to. This is essentially you buying a pension for yourself. Just make sure the payments are adjusted for inflation by making them mirror market funded indexes. That way the payments received can purchase the same amount at the start as they do years down the road.

what you need to be found and embraced! Laying out a budget and earning income are not things that only certain people can do. They are things that everyone should do! The knowledge to grow your wealth and eliminate debt can be found everywhere. You can learn from everyone in your life. Just look at what they do and where they are headed. Many people won't open up about finances but I feel that it is all the more reason to do it. Not only do I believe that anyone can be financially successful but I also believe that we should all be able to help each other get there too. It doesn't take much to lend a hand and make a difference in someone's life.

Follow the steps and envision your kingdom! Know where you are so you can start paving your path to where you want to be. You will earn your own throne by staying vigilant. Invest like crazy in order to earn your crown! Finally, once you get there. Never stop expanding your empire by continuing to learn about the paths ahead of you. We all can do this! So, if you haven't already started, start today!

Appendix

BUDGET TEMPLET

INCOME

INCOME #1	MONTHLY	ANNUALLY	INCOME #2	MONTHLY	ANNUALLY	INCOME #3	MONTHLY	ANNUALLY
TOTAL ENTITLEMENTS:			TOTAL ENTITLEMENTS:			TOTAL ENTITLEMENTS:		
DEDUCTIONS	MONTHLY	ANNUALLY	DEDUCTIONS	MONTHLY	ANNUALLY	DEDUCTIONS	MONTHLY	ANNUALLY
TOTAL DEDUCTIONS:			TOTAL DEDUCTIONS:			TOTAL DEDUCTIONS:		
NET INCOME:			NET INCOME:			NET INCOME:		

RENTAL PROPERTY:	MONTHLY	ANNUALLY
RENTAL INCOME:		
TAXES:		
NET GAIN:		

AFTER TAX INCOME:	MONTHLY	ANNUALLY

STANDARD SAVE FOR RETIREMENT		FINANCIAL INDEPENDENCE RETIRE EARLY	
HOUSING	30%	HOUSING	20%
FOOD	10%	FOOD	10%
SAVINGS	10%	SAVINGS	10%
INVESTMENT	15%	INVESTMENT	40%
MISC.	35%	MISC.	20%

HOME 20 - 30%	25%		MISC. 20 - 35%	28%		PERSONAL		
	MONTHLY	ANNUALLY	TRANSPORTATION	MONTHLY	ANNUALLY		MONTHLY	ANNUALLY
			TRANSPORTATION TOTAL:					
HOME TOTAL:			STREAMING	MONTHLY	ANNUALLY	PERSONAL TOTAL:		
FOOD 10% OR LESS	10%					LIVING	MONTHLY	ANNUALLY
	MONTHLY	ANNUALLY						
			STREAMING TOTAL:					
			CHARITABLE GIVING	MONTHLY	ANNUALLY			
						LIVING TOTAL:		
			CHARITABLE GIVING TOTAL:			MISC. TOTAL:		
FOOD TOTAL:			**TOTAL EXPENSES**					

OTHER ASSETS	VALUE
TOTAL	

DEBTS	VALUED AT	AMOUNT OWED	INTEREST	MONTHLY PAYMENT
TOTAL			**DIFFERENCE**	

PAY OFF PLAN

AMOUNT OWED		
PAYMENT		
MONTHS		EST. MONTHS OF INTEREST
		EST. YEARS UNTIL PAID
AMOUNT OWED		
PAYMENT		
MONTHS		EST. MONTHS OF INTEREST
		EST. YEARS UNTIL PAID
AMOUNT OWED		
PAYMENT		
MONTHS		EST. MONTHS OF INTEREST
		EST. YEARS UNTIL PAID

	SAVINGS 10%			MONTHLY	ANNUAL		
PRIORITY	TYPE OF FUND	MONTHLY INPUT	CURRENT FUNDS	ACCOUNT NAME	FULLY FUNDED	MONTHS UNTIL FUNDED	YEARS UNTIL FUNDED
1							
2							
3							
4							
5							
6							
7							
TOTALS				ALL:			

INVESTMENTS 15% (FIRE 40%+)		15%	40%	
PRIORITY	TYPE OF FUND	MONTHLY INPUT	CURRENT FUNDS	ACCOUNT NAME
1				
2				
3				
4				
5				
6				
7				
TOTALS				

Savings	$ -
Investments	$ -
Assets	$ -
Debts	$ -
CURRENT NET WORTH =	$ -

www.ingramcontent.com/pod-product-compliance
Lightning Source LLC
Chambersburg PA
CBHW051538120626
46551CB00013B/1276